P9-BYA-534

TURTLES, TOADS, and FROGS

A GOLDEN JUNIOR GUIDE™

TURTLES, TOADS, and FROGS

By GEORGE S. FICHTER
Illustrated by BARBARA HOOPES AMBLER

Consultant: Dr. Edmund D. Brodie, Jr., Professor and Chairman,
Department of Biology, The University of Texas at Arlington

A GOLDEN BOOK • NEW YORK
Western Publishing Company, Inc., Racine, Wisconsin 53404

Turtles are reptiles. So are snakes, lizards, and alligators. All of these cold-blooded animals have a backbone. But a turtle's body is also enclosed in a protective shell. The part of the shell covering the turtle's back is called the *carapace*. The part underneath the animal is called the *plastron*. In the following pages, you will meet some of the most familiar or commonly seen turtles.

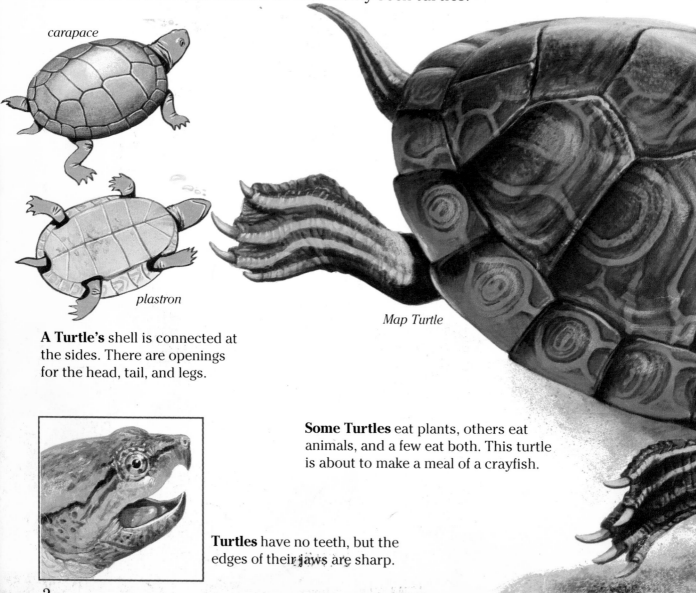

carapace

plastron

Map Turtle

A Turtle's shell is connected at the sides. There are openings for the head, tail, and legs.

Some Turtles eat plants, others eat animals, and a few eat both. This turtle is about to make a meal of a crayfish.

Turtles have no teeth, but the edges of their jaws are sharp.

Did You Know?
Baby turtles look just like tiny adults.

Female Turtles
lay eggs in piles of leaves or holes dug in sand or dirt.

Eastern Box Turtle

eggs

hatchlings

young turtle

Tortoises

Tortoises are turtles that live on land. They usually have a more rounded, or domed, shell than do sea or freshwater turtles. Their front legs are club-shaped, and their hind legs are thick and stumpy, like an elephant's. Tortoises are strictly plant eaters.

A Tortoise's shell has *growth rings* on it. These cannot be counted to tell a tortoise's exact age, the way the rings on tree trunks can. But the older the tortoise is, the more rings it has.

growth rings

Desert Tortoises

Did You Know?
Tortoises live a long time. Some have been known to reach the age of 150 years or more!

Gopher Tortoise burrow

Gopher Tortoise

Gopher Tortoises hide in burrows when not grazing on plants. Their cool underground homes may be 12 feet long.

Did You Also Know?
Tortoises move very slowly. Even when they hurry, they do not go very fast. It would take a tortoise an hour to walk a city block!

Box Turtles eat mainly fruits, flowers, and leaves. But they will also eat worms, insects, and other small animals.

Western Box Turtle

Box Turtles live on land, too. When they need to protect themselves, they can pull their legs, neck, and head completely inside their hard shell. Then they close the shell up tight. This makes it very hard for other animals to bite them! Box Turtles are usually very gentle. They are sometimes kept as pets.

Did You Know?
Box Turtles can eat poisonous mushrooms without harm. But the poison is stored in the body. If another animal eats the turtle, it may die.

The Male Box Turtle's eyes are bright red. The female's are reddish brown. The male's tail is also longer than the female's.

male *female*

7

Green Turtles

Green Turtles are sea turtles. Like all sea turtles, they live in the ocean. Green turtles come on land only to lay their eggs. Females crawl slowly up the beach to beyond the water's edge. There they dig a hole, or nest, in the sand and lay as many as 200 eggs. They cover the eggs with sand. Then they make their way back to the sea. Males never leave the ocean.

Green Turtle laying eggs

Baby Sea Turtles crawl out of the nest right after hatching. They head to the sea. They know how to swim without being taught!

hatchlings heading out to sea

Did You Know?

The Loggerhead and the Hawksbill are two other sea turtles. The Hawksbill, at less than 3 feet, is the smallest sea turtle. On its back is the famous "tortoise shell" pattern, often copied to make jewelry, eyeglass frames, and other decorative items.

All Sea Turtles are endangered. They were once hunted heavily for food. Also, many of the beaches where they nested have been destroyed.

Green Turtle

Leatherbacks

Leatherbacks are the largest of the sea turtles. They can be up to 8 feet long and weigh 2,000 pounds! A Leatherback's shell is leathery rather than bony. It feels like a wet shoe. The shell has ridges on the back and sides.

ridge

Leatherback Turtle

A Sea Turtle's legs are like flippers. They are good for swimming but not very good for walking on land.

sea turtle's leg

land turtle's leg

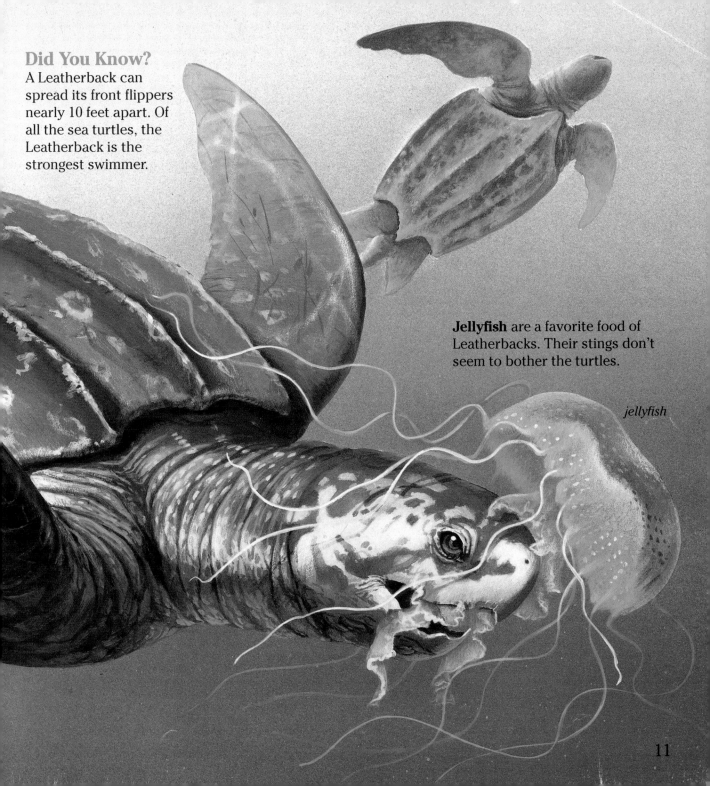

Did You Know?
A Leatherback can spread its front flippers nearly 10 feet apart. Of all the sea turtles, the Leatherback is the strongest swimmer.

Jellyfish are a favorite food of Leatherbacks. Their stings don't seem to bother the turtles.

jellyfish

11

Softshelled Turtles

Softshelled Turtles live in fresh water instead of in the sea. But like Leatherbacks, they have a soft, leathery shell covering their body. Some have short, sharp spines on their back. All have a long, snakelike neck and a tube-shaped snout. The snout is used like a snorkel for breathing. Softshelled Turtles are quick to bite.

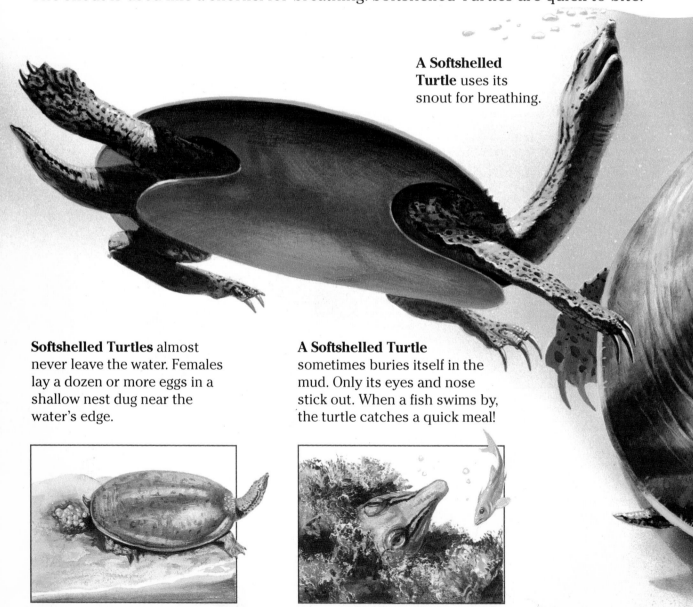

A Softshelled Turtle uses its snout for breathing.

Softshelled Turtles almost never leave the water. Females lay a dozen or more eggs in a shallow nest dug near the water's edge.

A Softshelled Turtle sometimes buries itself in the mud. Only its eyes and nose stick out. When a fish swims by, the turtle catches a quick meal!

Spiny Softshelled Turtle

The Spiny Softshelled Turtle is the largest of the three kinds of Softshelled Turtles found in the United States. Some females are more than 1½ feet long, about the size of a newborn human baby. Males are only half as big as females.

13

Snappers, also called Snapping Turtles, are quick-tempered. They lash out, or strike at enemies, with the speed of a snake. Once their powerful, sharp-edged jaws snap shut, they will not let go. Snapping Turtles eat fish and other animals they catch in the water.

Common Snappers may weigh more than 80 pounds. However, most are much smaller. Look for them in ponds, lakes, or streams.

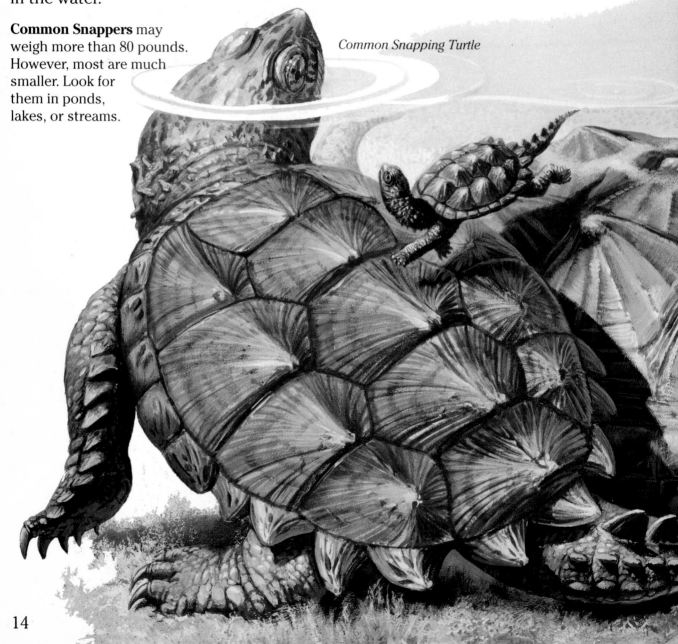

Common Snapping Turtle

Alligator Snapping Turtle

An Alligator Snapper that is hungry opens its mouth and wiggles a pink, wormlike "lure" on the tip of its tongue. If a fish swims inside to get this bait, the turtle snaps its jaws shut. Then it swallows the fish.

Did You Know?

Both Musk and Mud Turtles give off a strong, unpleasant odor if disturbed or frightened. In fact, Musk Turtles smell so bad, they are often called *Stinkpots.*

"Stinkpot" Musk Turtle

ridge

Musk Turtles usually have a ridge down the middle of their back.

Musk and Mud Turtles

Musk and Mud Turtles stay in the water nearly all the time. You are most likely to see them crawling along the shallow bottom of a pond or lake. To hide, they draw their head and long neck inside their shell. If another animal bothers them, they will suddenly stick their head out and try to bite the intruder.

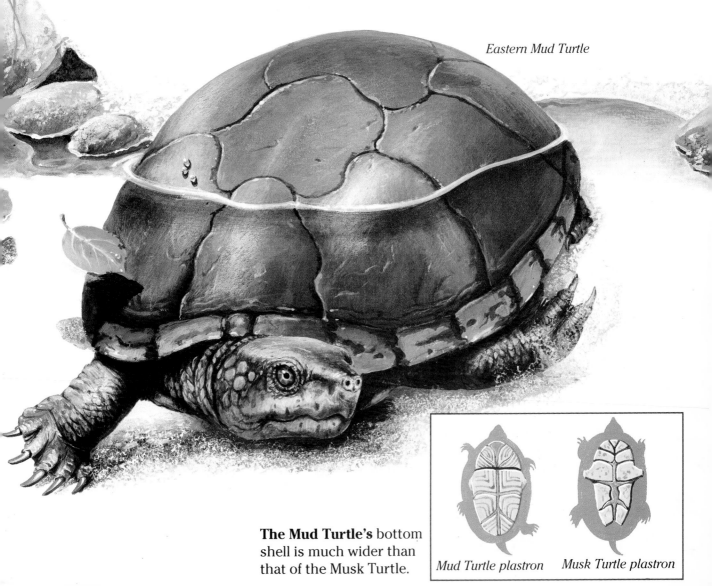

Eastern Mud Turtle

The Mud Turtle's bottom shell is much wider than that of the Musk Turtle.

Mud Turtle plastron   *Musk Turtle plastron*

17

Painted Turtles
can be found sunning themselves on rocks and logs and along the shores of ponds, lakes, and streams. But you must be quick (and quiet!) to catch sight of them. They are very timid. At the slightest sound they plunge into the water and disappear. Painted Turtles rarely grow bigger than 5 inches long.

Midland Painted Turtle

Painted Turtles have webs between their toes. This is true of all turtles that spend a lot of time in water. Webs help by pushing water out behind the animal as it swims.

Eastern Painted Turtle

web

18

Did You Know?
Because of their bright colors and calm nature, Painted Turtles are often kept as pets.

Western Painted Turtle

Southern Painted Turtle

Did You Also Know?
All aquatic turtles, including Painted Turtles, swallow their food underwater.

19

Toads and Frogs

Toads and Frogs are amphibians. The word *amphibian* means "living a double life." Most frogs and toads spend part of their lives in water and part on land. Most also have tiny, sharp teeth that help them hold on to struggling prey. The young, called *tadpoles,* breathe through gills, like fish. Adults have lungs and breathe air. They may also take in oxygen through their skin. Tadpoles eat mostly plants. Adults feed mainly on insects. In the pages that follow you'll meet some of the most familiar or commonly seen species.

Did You Know?

The "ears" of a frog or toad are called the *tympani.* They are flat, round disks. Like our own eardrums, these disks vibrate in response to a sound. This is how the frog or toad hears.

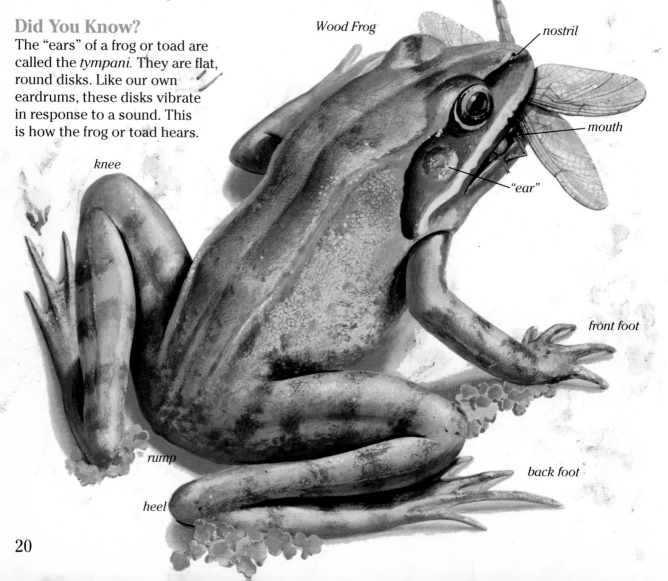

Wood Frog

nostril

mouth

"ear"

knee

front foot

rump

back foot

heel

20

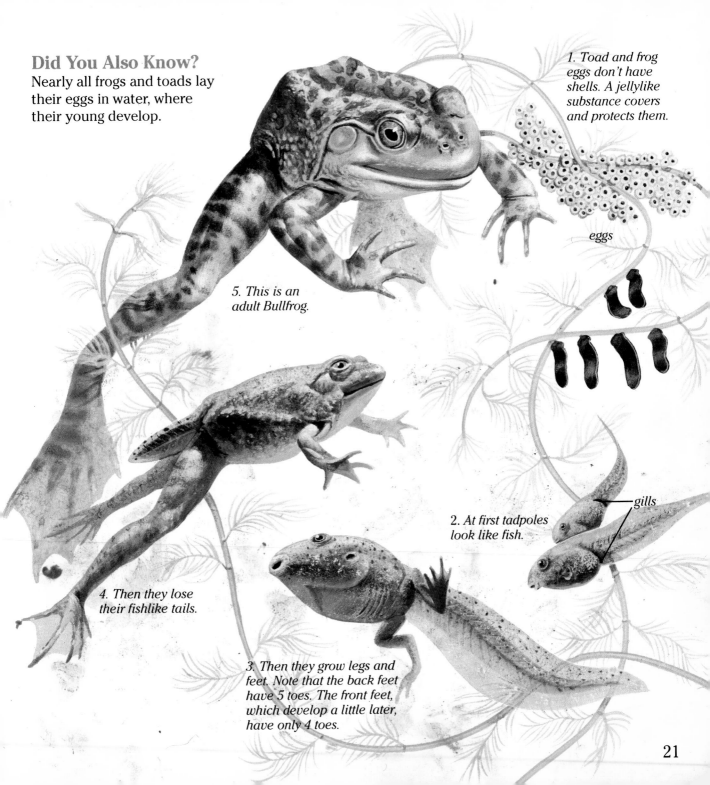

Did You Also Know?
Nearly all frogs and toads lay their eggs in water, where their young develop.

1. Toad and frog eggs don't have shells. A jellylike substance covers and protects them.

eggs

5. This is an adult Bullfrog.

gills

2. At first tadpoles look like fish.

4. Then they lose their fishlike tails.

3. Then they grow legs and feet. Note that the back feet have 5 toes. The front feet, which develop a little later, have only 4 toes.

21

Is It a Toad or a Frog?

Neither toads nor frogs have tails. Both lay eggs, and their young, the tadpoles, develop in water. But there are important differences between the two.

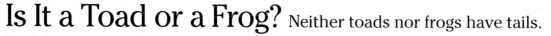

Frogs
- ❑ Frogs have a streamlined body.
- ❑ A frog's skin is moist and smooth.
- ❑ Frogs do not have bumps on their head.
- ❑ Frogs jump—sometimes several times the length of their body.
- ❑ Frogs lay their eggs in a clump.

Green Frog

Did You Know?
Toads and frogs usually shed their skin every week or so. They eat the old skin.

Most Toads and Frogs have their tongue attached to the front, rather than to the back, of the mouth.

Toads

- ❏ Toads have a plump body.
- ❏ A toad's skin is dry and warty.
- ❏ Toads have a large bump (poison gland) just behind each "ear."
- ❏ Toads hop, though only a few inches at a time.
- ❏ Toads lay their eggs in a string.

poison gland

Woodhouse's Toad

"ear"

23

Marine Toads

Marine Toads are the giants of the toad family, measuring up to 9 inches long. They are found in warm climates throughout the world. Farmers like them because they eat lots of insects. This helps to protect the crops. Like many toads, Marine Toads usually have a faint line down the middle of their back.

Toads do not cause warts. But when threatened, they do give off a milky fluid from the wartlike bumps on their back. This same fluid is released by the big poison gland behind each "ear." The secretion stings and tastes awful. It can even be deadly. Dogs, foxes, raccoons, and other predators quickly spit out a toad after taking a bite.

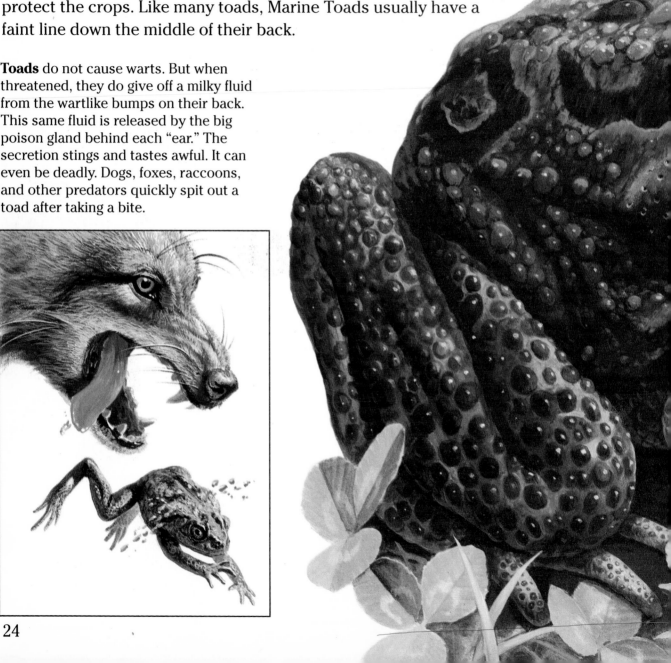

Marine Toad

poison gland

"ear"

A Marine Toad can eat 50 crickets—or hundreds of flies—in just 10 minutes!

Did You Know?
Touching a toad can be painful! Always wash your hands after picking up a toad. This will get rid of the stinging secretions from the toad's glands.

25

American Toads

American Toads spend most of their time on land, but they never go far from water. Many are brownish, but some are almost gray. The spots on their body are often red or orange. American Toads eat many insects. That is why people like having them in their yards and gardens.

Did You Know?
A toad's color often matches the color of the soil where it lives.

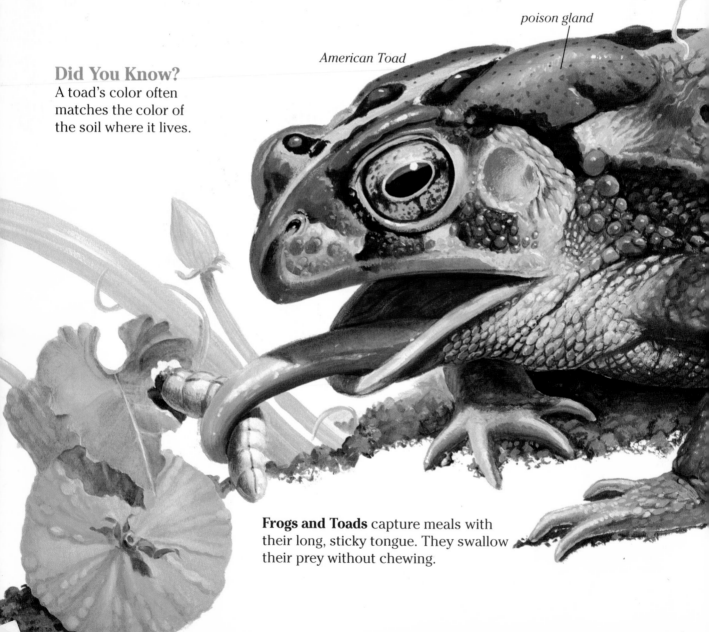

poison gland

American Toad

Frogs and Toads capture meals with their long, sticky tongue. They swallow their prey without chewing.

Male Frogs and Toads can usually "sing." They do this by blowing up a pouch in their throat. Their trills and chirps are used to attract mates. You can learn to recognize different kinds of frogs or toads by their calls.

throat pouch blown up

27

Spadefoot Toads,

Spadefoot Toads, which most scientists now believe are really frogs, live in the hot desert. They escape the heat and dryness by digging into the sand—backward! Using the "spades" on their hind feet, they can dig so rapidly that they sink out of sight in a flash. They may come out at night to feed. But during dry spells they stay underground.

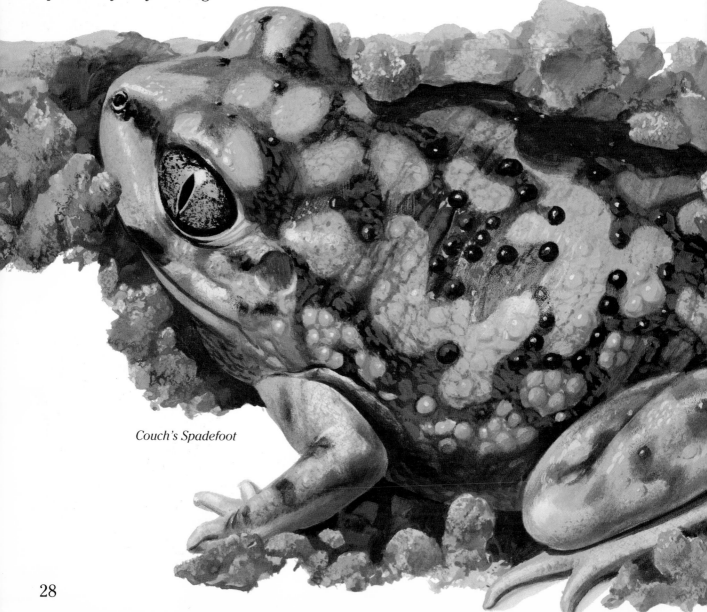

Couch's Spadefoot

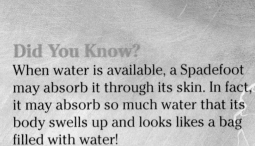

Did You Know?

When water is available, a Spadefoot may absorb it through its skin. In fact, it may absorb so much water that its body swells up and looks likes a bag filled with water!

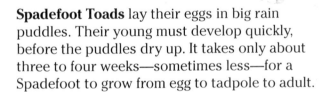

Spadefoot Toads lay their eggs in big rain puddles. Their young must develop quickly, before the puddles dry up. It takes only about three to four weeks—sometimes less—for a Spadefoot to grow from egg to tadpole to adult.

"spade" on hind foot

Bullfrogs

Bullfrogs are the largest frogs in the United States. Males grow up to 8 inches long. A Bullfrog has huge "ears," the flat, round disks on the sides of its head. The male's "ears" are much larger than the female's. Bullfrogs call to each other when they are looking for mates. They make deep, echoing sounds. Favorite foods include mice, birds, snakes, small turtles—even other frogs!

male Bullfrog

"ear"

The Male Bullfrog's loud calls are heard in the spring and also after warm summer rains.

30

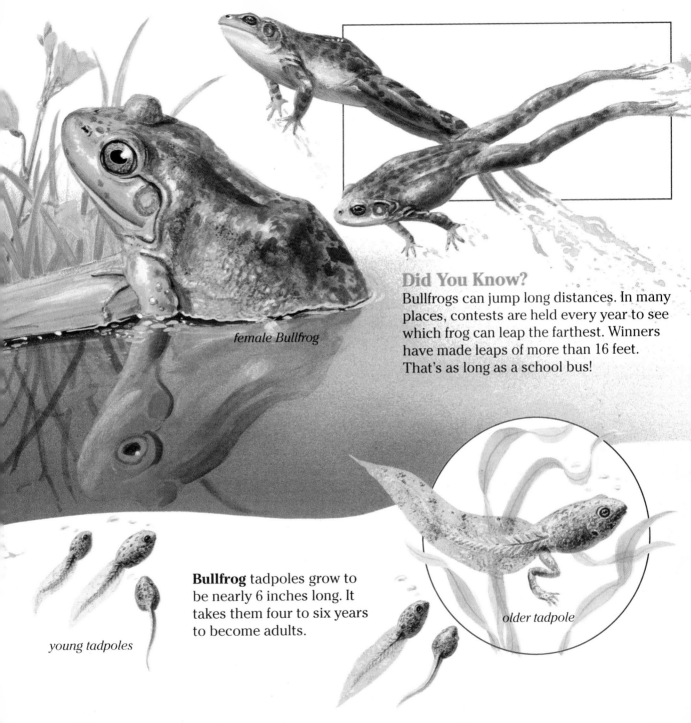

female Bullfrog

Did You Know?

Bullfrogs can jump long distances. In many places, contests are held every year to see which frog can leap the farthest. Winners have made leaps of more than 16 feet. That's as long as a school bus!

Bullfrog tadpoles grow to be nearly 6 inches long. It takes them four to six years to become adults.

young tadpoles

older tadpole

Leopard Frogs were once common in wetlands and along the shores of many U.S. ponds, lakes, and streams. Now they are rare, as are many amphibians. This is mainly because their *habitats* (homes in the wild) have been destroyed or become polluted.

Leopard Frogs may be either green or brown. They have many round, dark spots on their bodies—like leopards.

Leopard Frog

Pickerel Frogs are similar to Leopard Frogs. But their spots are square or rectangular in shape.

Pickerel Frog

33

Treefrogs have a suction pad at the end of each toe. Using these pads, they can easily climb trees and rocks—even smooth panes of glass! These frogs produce very loud, trilling calls by blowing up their throat pouch. They announce the arrival of spring with their calls, some of which sound just like birdcalls!

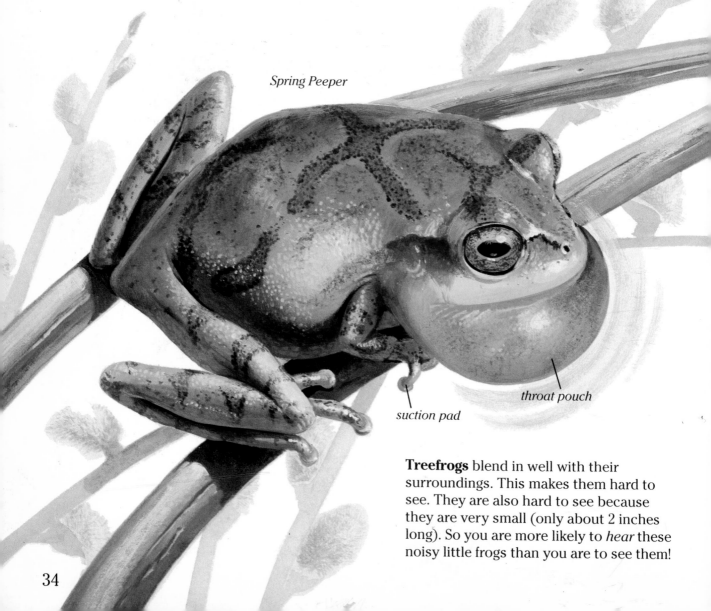

Spring Peeper

suction pad

throat pouch

Treefrogs blend in well with their surroundings. This makes them hard to see. They are also hard to see because they are very small (only about 2 inches long). So you are more likely to *hear* these noisy little frogs than you are to see them!

Common Gray Treefrogs

Common Gray Treefrogs may have either gray or green skin.

Western Chorus Frog

Chorus Frogs are similar to Treefrogs in size. In the spring, when they are looking for mates, they are as noisy as Treefrogs. Some have pads on their toes, too. But Chorus Frogs cannot climb as well as Treefrogs.

35

For Further Reading

With this book, you've only just begun to explore some exciting new worlds. Why not continue to learn about the creatures known as turtles, toads, and frogs? For example, you might want to browse through *Reptiles and Amphibians (Golden Guide),* which contains many fascinating details on the animals in this book and additional ones as well. Also, be sure to visit your local library, where you will discover a variety of titles on the subject. Two other Golden Books you might enjoy are: *I Wonder If Dragons Are Real and Other Neat Facts About Reptiles and Amphibians* and *The Golden Book of Snakes and Other Reptiles.*

Index